CW00498263

The Boy Who Was Different Growing Up

Daniel Hinnigan

A special thank you to...

Mr Mansfield for inspiring me to write another book.

Mrs Holmes, Mrs Jenkins, Mrs Grace (Assistant SENCO), Miss McDonald, Mrs Stephenson, Mrs Grace (Form Teacher), Miss Crickett, Mr Flowers , Mrs Fay, Mr Hepworth, Mrs Price, Gail Jessop, Matthew Crane, Luke Cooney, Daniel Brady, all of my friends and my wonderful family.

Especially my incredible Mum and Dad.

Thank you everyone!

Please be aware that most of the names in this story are fictional due to personal reasons...

Introduction

Jude had finally survived 2 years in secondary school by now and he couldn't believe he done it. Jude was just looking forward to the summer holidays. He was happy to relax for a few weeks and not worry about anything to do with school until September.

So the pieces of the puzzle were all stuck together but not with the strongest of glues, so they would probably fall apart soon...

Part 1:

It had come to the 6th of September and it was now time for Jude to start Year 9 and he was pretty nervous; due to the changes, the new GCSE courses, picking his options and growing up a little more.

At the beginning of Year 9, Jude was very excited for what the new school year had to bring. He never felt very excited over Year 7 or 8 – in fact, he was absolutely terrified when he started Year 7. But that was then, this is now. Well, sort of.

I think Jude was excited because he was making a pretty big decision about his options and it was the last year of Key - Stage 3. He felt like maybe if he was starting Year 10 in a year he could be trusted to be more independent.

But Jude was just day – dreaming. He wasn't really independent anyway. He never went out with friends because he felt like he wouldn't 'fit in' with them outside of school and he was actually quite embarrassed that he never went out and left it this late, so he never went out at all. Jude doesn't really have much in common with the people who he talks to in school because they all like football and a load of other things Jude doesn't take any interest in. He has some things in common with them, but not a lot. People may think he is 'anti-social' but he doesn't mean it, Jude struggles to 'fit in' with other people sometimes. He just left it and never worried or even thought about it.

Jude was also really happy because his brother Eric and his girlfriend Eva were expecting their first child, a little girl. Jude was going to become an uncle. This made Jude really happy, and really excited; to excited actually, he never shut up about the baby! He didn't know if it was a good thing or not. He kept on going on and on about the baby, he thought too himself *'I am annoying Eva by blabbing on or is it just me?'*

He was wondering if he could by a bib with the baby scan on saying: 'MY UNCLE …… IS THE BEST!'

(The ……'S meaning something else!) But he would've never got away with it. So he bought a baby bath instead. So the baby, the accomplishment of 2 years in 'BIG SCHOOL' and that's it. Everything should be positive, for now.

Even though Jude was pretty happy about Year 9, he had a few changes to deal with but he dealt with them (in a very awkward and weird way, Jude's way, which wasn't the best of ways to deal with things). Jude doesn't like changes, when his formal routine gets messed around he feels vulnerable and gets stressed out. Jude's timetable didn't change a lot so he was happy about that but he had a few new teachers who he didn't really know. Miss Harley, she taught him ICT. Jude didn't really understand her and she probably didn't understand him. So he became stressed because he couldn't keep up in class as he didn't understand the teacher and how she taught the lesson. He actually refused to go to her lessons in the end because he couldn't cope with all of the

stress. A few weeks later, Jude grew up a little more and they finally got on with each other - they still get on to this day.

As time passed by Jude was having more problems, but with other people in school. He was getting blamed for reading confidential letters when he wasn't and was confused in the fact why someone would lie and deliberately upset him. So he 'went off on one' when he was told this. He was told off due to his angriness, tone of voice and the way he was in school but he was just confused, that's all. The teacher wasn't the very best of help because she even believed

 the lie and shouted at Jude.

Jude doesn't like people shouting, if someone shouts at him, he will either tell them to stop shouting or he will shout back. When Jude gets shouted at or

he is in the same room when people are shouting he usually covers his ears or walks out. Now if you were walking past you would probably think that he is being cheeky but he isn't, he just doesn't like the noise.

Jude was also having a hard time with his Dad. They were arguing every time they saw each other and Jude was just sick of it. It's natural for Jude and his Dad to moan and argue with one another every now and again because they're so alike, but this time they were arguing all the time.

His dad was winding him up and annoying him and Jude could not keep all of that in, so he used to argue back with his dad! This caused an awkward atmosphere in the house, well for Jude anyway.

Jude was confused with his dad. Sometimes he was kind, nice and happy. The next minute he would be angry, grumpy and he would start moaning at him. Jude just

10

began thinking that it was because he was getting older and so was his dad.

Jude had developed a tick, by nodding his head; and his Dad was telling him off every time he nodded his head.

Jude was wondering in the end if his Dad didn't understand why he had the tick so that was why he was telling him off, but he didn't know, so he gave up thinking.

People were also making fun of him in school over it as well, the people who he classed as his 'friends'. This was an isolated period for Jude. These 'friends' of Jude were making fun of his nickname 'Rainman'

– he was only called that because he can remember most events in his life, sometimes he could even remember the TV guide, presenters on shows, or what he was doing exactly a week, month or year ago.

He just ignored all of that and 'bottled it up' when it happened again. *So what's the difference here then?*

After all of the negativity, Jude was really proud of himself, he was writing stories about his life with Asperger's, his first story was published on an autistic blog and was getting used in his English lessons. He was proud of this because it was something he done all by himself (but with some help of his English teacher and others of course.) It took guts to write, because he wasn't sure if it was going to turn out the way he imagined it to.

Jude was praised by all his teachers, well most of them anyway. He was very happy with himself, so were his family.

After all of that positivity, Jude felt blue. He didn't know why at first but then he worked out that he was upset over Val. The greatest person who was like a Nan to him.

He just used to start crying over the bereavement and get so upset. Val had three daughters, who Jude used to call his aunties because they were so close. They used to call him their nephew too. But when Val tragically passed away, Jude never used to see them or speak to them as he used to. As this was a big and difficult

13

change for Jude it made him so upset because he used to see them nearly every day; and he didn't anymore. But he was told that Val was like the person who held everyone together, the main magnet, and when Val went, everyone just drifted apart. It hurt Jude every day and it still does but it always will because unfortunately, life isn't what it's made out to be.

He passes Val's house twice a day, where one of her daughters still lives. He wants to knock and talk to them but he feels scared. He has them on Facebook and they still like and comment on his posts sometimes but it's not the same.

He just kept it all to himself at first because he felt so embarrassed of the fact that a thirteen year old boy was so upset all the time.

14

A few weeks later, Jude's fourteenth birthday arrived. Everyone always asks him if he feels different on his birthday, he just used to think in his mind 'really? '- Jude always felt different, he still does. But on Jude's birthday he invites some of his family down so he can see them so everyone can be together on a happy day. A week later, Jude went out with Val's daughters for his birthday and he slept in their house. He thought that this would've brought everyone back together, *but guess what? It didn't.* Jude felt very awkward because it was just him, his mum, sister or brothers didn't go with them and he felt quite 'sly on them'. But in the end he moved on and never thought about it.

The struggle with the bereavement wasn't the only problem though. Jude had to cope with even more changes due to teachers being absent and room changes all the time. He had a new teacher who he absolutely HATED! Despite the touching incident, they just didn't get along, he didn't understand his teaching (well, nobody did really), but he couldn't control

his class so everything was too loud for Jude and this made Jude so stressed and angry he just ignored the teacher. This wasn't the best of actions to really.

In fact it made things worse, very worse. Jude was a little cheeky but it was only how he was feeling at the time because when Jude was confused about the work, the teacher used to ignore him and tell him off for not listening. This drove Jude MAD!

Jude was just sick of going to this certain teacher's lessons and didn't want to go anymore.

Jude was thinking what the point in life was if everyone is just horrible to each other...

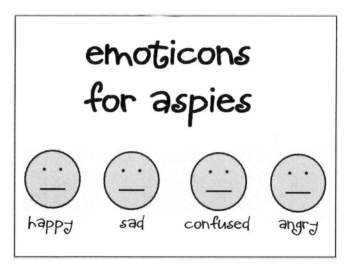

Part 2:

A few months later, Jude's brother's baby was born *(that didn't take long did it?)* Baby Autumn, Jude was so happy. He was always happy when he saw her, she always cheered him up.

Jude was thinking if baby Autumn would've brought everyone back together; but no, that wasn't the case, he was still upset but he wasn't angry at the baby; he just thought that may have happened. Jude felt very happy that the baby was here. He loved seeing her in the bath he bought her, it made him proud when he saw her using the gift her bought for her.

Now through all of the happiness, Jude was still upset. The worst thing was that he never told anyone. He bottled it all up!

Jude was still struggling; he was just getting upset all the time and he used to break-down every time he went passed Val's house. If he was on the bus laughing and messing around with his friends, as soon as he would go passed he just used to stop and go silent. His friends didn't get on to it because he never told them so they just carried on.

As time went on, it was now time for Jude to choose his options. He picked an I.T. course called CiDA and Geography *(as he could only pick two)*. He was quite happy with them choices, so he wasn't worrying about it.

A week later an autism awareness week was taking place in the UK and Jude wanted to have an autism awareness week in school. So he approached his head of year and the head teacher. He was allowed to organize it so he printed off posters, had a competition, made an assembly and collected some charity money. He did this with the help of some teachers of course. He felt very happy with himself because he was doing something to spread awareness of autism.

About a month later, Jude had his first book published on Amazon. This was a great achievement for Jude. Everyone praised him; they were all so interested about Jude's story. But (again), it wasn't all 'top – notch'. He didn't really tell anyone but some people were putting him down over the book.

Some boys in his school were asking him so many questions about it such as: '*How*

many pages'? *'Why did you write it'?* He
then answered them and they laughed and
replied *with 'it's not a real book because
he's just desperate or nobody likes it they're
all just lying'.* Jude got really stressed and
angry because he felt like he could've done
more. He was now putting himself down
over his greatest achievement. The worst
thing somebody said to him was that only
his mum and dad would buy the book to
have some buyers because they felt sly on
him! This made Jude furious.

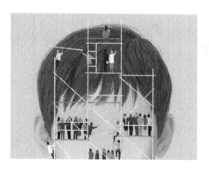

Other people were embarrassing him saying
'he is really different because he was
writing books and he was just being stupid
for writing books'. Other people from
different schools were then asking him why

he wrote the book and Jude just felt so embarrassed. He went red-faced.

What do you think he did?

Oh, well; he bottled it all up AGAIN!

Jude started thinking again. They must just be jealous of him because he has done something with his life or because he is standing up for him and other people with autism.

He proved them all wrong because a lot of people bought his book and he even had an interview in the school magazine. He was so proud of himself after all of that because he was opening up about his diagnosis with Asperger's. He was even told that once he opened up, a few other boys in his year opened up as well. So his book did make a difference.

The general election was coming up and Jude always had something to say. He's interested in politics, his step-mum is a Labour councillor and he always helped her and the other councillors out, even the MP. He was going door-knocking, leafleting and phoning people up from the office and this even made a difference.

When the general election was over and he stopped campaigning, Jude received a letter from the MP herself and in the letter it read; '*Thank you for all of your help throughout the campaigning for the general election*'. Jude just lit up when he read the letter, he just felt so positive.

Now after all of the positivity there was just a dark storm heading its way up to Jude's mind...

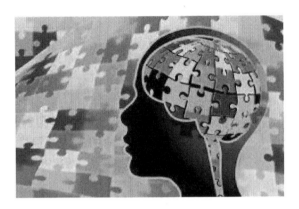

When Jude 'bottles things up' he doesn't tell anyone at all. So he felt like he needed to do something and one day he was fed up and all of the things he had bottled up just came bursting out of him. Jude was feeling pretty down and he just lost control of himself and his own feelings.

Jude was feeling so down that he made a silly decision and he knows now that it was the wrong thing to do because it upset a lot of people. It's a common thing for anyone to feel down but not everyone goes down the way Jude did. If you do ever feel the same or you have then talk to someone, anyone because Jude didn't and he had to realise the hard way that he had to talk to someone before it was too late. He was unable to focus on anything as he went through it on his own until he eventually spoke to someone and found some help.

Jude tried really hard to forget about that dark week but he just couldn't, he still tries really hard now. But he just knows he will never forget because it happened and it can't be erased from his life.

It had now come to an end of Year 9 and Jude was definitely ready for the summer break. Jude wanted to use his spare time to focus writing on his second book and reflect on the school year he had.

Jude had written the first part of his second book just 3 weeks in to the summer break. He wanted to inform and aware even more people about autism by writing books every few months.

The summer break continued and Jude was getting very nervous about going back to school. He was nervous of going back to school because he was starting an important year in school and he was so scared of messing things up. He was just thinking ahead and overthinking everything. Jude always does this when he's nervous and when he overthinks things he gets put off and gets anxious.

But Jude had let the school situation go – for now anyway...

The summer holidays had passed *(very quickly)* and it came to the last week of the summer break and Jude had a decision to make. There was a music festival near the area Jude lives and Jude's Step-mum had bought tickets. He wanted to go but he doesn't like crowds and loud noises. Jude gets very anxious and starts to worry when there are a lot of people surrounding him. He was trying very hard to make the decision, so he slept on it.

He then decided to go because its life, you only live once and he wants to live life without any ifs or but's *(well, that's what Jude wants to do anyway, for now)*...

27

So the pieces of the puzzle all fell apart for Jude again but they were stuck back together with stronger glue for now. Will they be stuck together forever or will the glue become weak again soon?

Author: Daniel Hinnigan

Daniel Hinnigan is a teenage boy from Liverpool and this is his second book. He has Asperger Syndrome and Jude is a metaphorical character based upon Daniel.

Daniel is educated in Saint Francis Xavier's College in Woolton, Liverpool. He is currently studying the subjects in his GCSE

course. He recently had an interview on a local Radio station about his first book and raising awareness of Asperger's.

Daniel also won a very special award at his Schools Proclamation ceremony recently for his books, raising awareness of Asperger's, helping in the school Library and helping 'The Labour Party' posting leaflets, door knocking and phone canvassing.

He hopes that everyone will be aware of autism in years to come – this is why he is writing stories based upon him living and coping with Asperger Syndrome.

Daniel's next book will be based upon how Jude copes with life in his GCSE course from Year 10 to 11...

If you haven't read Daniel's first book 'The Boy Who Was Different' then why don't you?

It's available on amazon for £5.

Coming soon:

'What do I know about Asperger Syndrome?' - 2018

'The Boy Who Was Different Moving On' - 2019

Printed in Great Britain
by Amazon